Spark Your Fire

"A Guide to Igniting Your Inner Flame"

BY

M.J.MOON

It is creative nonfiction, in this case. For various reasons, several parts have undergone variable degrees of fictionalization.

Copyright © M.J.MOON, 2024

Except for reviewers who may cite brief sections in reviews, no part of this book may be duplicated in any way without the publisher's prior written consent by any mechanical or electronic means, including information storage and retrieval systems.

Table of Contents

Disclaimer 6

Chapter 1 7

The Fire Within 7

1.1   Motivation 8

1.2   The Discovering Your Spark 9

1.3   Power of Mindset 11

1.4   Overcoming Obstacles 13

Chapter 2 16

Goal Setting and Achievement 16

2.1 Setting SMART Goals 17

2.2 Creating a Roadmap 20

2.3 Staying Focused and Motivated 22

2.4 Celebrating Success 24

Chapter 3 27

Building a Support System 27

3.1 The Importance of Relationships 28

3.2 Finding Your Tribe 30

3.3 Seeking Help 32

3.4 The Power of Giving Back 34

Chapter 4 36

Self-Care and Well-being 36

4.1 Taking Care of Yourself 37

4.2 Stress Management Techniques 39

4.3 Healthy Habits 40

4.4 Finding Balance 42

Chapter 5 44

Inspiring Stories and Role Models 44

5.1 The Power of Inspiration 45

5.2 Famous Role Models 46

5.3 Everyday Heroes 48

5.4 Becoming Your Own Hero 50

Conclusion 52

Disclaimer

This book is intended to provide motivation, inspiration, and practical advice for young adults. The stories and examples included are based on real-life experiences, but names, details, and circumstances may have been altered to protect privacy and confidentiality. While the author has made every effort to ensure the accuracy of the information provided, this book is not a substitute for professional advice. Readers are encouraged to seek appropriate professional guidance when needed. The author and publisher are not responsible for any action's individuals take based on the information in this book.

Chapter 1

The Fire Within

1.1 Motivation

Motivation is the driving force that propels us towards our goals. The inner spark ignites our desire to achieve, learn, and grow. Motivation can come from various sources, but it's essentially the reason why we do what we do.

There are two main types of motivation: **Intrinsic Motivation:** This comes from within ourselves.
It's the feeling of satisfaction, enjoyment, or purpose that we derive from an activity itself. For example, someone might be intrinsically motivated to play the guitar because they love the music and the feeling of creating something.

Extrinsic Motivation: This comes from external factors, such as rewards, praise, or avoidance of punishment. For instance, a student might be extrinsically motivated to study hard to get good grades and avoid failing. While both types of motivation can be helpful, intrinsic motivation is often more sustainable and fulfilling. When we are intrinsically motivated, we are more likely to persist in our efforts, even when faced with challenges.

Motivation plays a crucial role in achieving our goals. It gives us the energy, focus, and determination needed to overcome obstacles and persevere through setbacks. Without motivation, it can be challenging to maintain the drive and commitment required to succeed.

1.2 The Discovering Your Spark

Finding your "spark" is about identifying what truly excites and inspires you. It's about discovering what makes your heart race and your eyes light up. Your spark is your unique passion, which drives you to be your best.

To help you discover your spark, try these exercises:

Reflect on your childhood: Think about the activities you enjoyed as a child. Were there any hobbies or interests that you were particularly passionate about?

Identify your strengths: What are you naturally good at? What do you find easy or enjoyable?

Explore your values: What is important to you in life? What values do you want to live by?

Imagine your ideal life: What would it look like if you could live any life you wanted? What would you be doing?

The Importance of Following Your Passion

Following your passion is more than just a hobby or interest; it's a powerful force that can profoundly shape your life. Pursuing your love makes you more likely to experience a deep sense of fulfillment and satisfaction. Engaging in activities you love can boost your mood, reduce stress, and improve your overall well-being. Passion acts as a powerful motivator. When you're genuinely interested in something, you're more likely to stay committed and persevere through challenges. Pursuing your passion can lead to personal growth and development. You'll learn new skills, expand your knowledge, and discover your strengths and weaknesses.

1.3 Power of Mindset

Mindset refers to our beliefs about our abilities and potential. It's essentially our perspective on ourselves and our capabilities. There are two main types of mindsets:

Fixed Mindset: People with a fixed mindset believe their abilities are innate and unchangeable. They tend to see challenges as obstacles that they can't overcome.

Growth Mindset: People with a growth mindset believe their abilities can be developed through effort and practice. They view challenges as opportunities to learn and grow. A growth mindset is crucial for enhancing motivation. When we believe that we can improve and develop our skills, we're more likely to be motivated to put in the effort required to achieve our goals.

Strategies to Develop a Growth Mindset

A growth mindset is essential for personal and professional Success. Here are some effective strategies to cultivate this mindset:

Challenge Negative Thoughts: Pay attention to your thoughts and identify any negative self-talk that might limit your beliefs. Instead of telling yourself, "I can't do this," try saying, "I can learn and improve." Instead of focusing solely on the outcome, focus on the process of learning and improving.

Embrace Challenges: Instead of seeing challenges as obstacles, view them as opportunities for growth and learning. Make challenges seem less daunting by breaking them down into smaller, more manageable steps.
Celebrate Progress: No matter how small, celebrate your progress and accomplishments. Reward yourself for reaching milestones or overcoming challenges. Track your progress and reflect on your achievements.
Practice Self-Compassion: Treat yourself with kindness and understanding. Instead of beating yourself up for mistakes, focus on learning and improving.

By incorporating these strategies into your daily life, you can develop a growth mindset and unlock your full potential. Remember, it's a journey, and progress may not always be linear. Stay patient, persistent, and committed to your growth.

1.4 Overcoming Obstacles

Young adults often face various challenges that can hinder their motivation and progress. Some common obstacles are Fear of failure, rejection, or the unknown, which can be a significant barrier to achieving goals. Doubting one's abilities or worth can undermine motivation and confidence. Putting off tasks or avoiding responsibilities can lead to stress, anxiety, and decreased productivity.

Overcoming Obstacles: Strategies for Success

Overcoming obstacles is a common challenge that everyone faces at some point in their lives. Here are some effective strategies to help you overcome challenges and achieve your goals:

Identify the Obstacle: Clearly identify the obstacle that is hindering your progress. Determine the underlying reasons for the obstacle.

Develop a Plan: Break down the obstacle into smaller, more manageable goals. Set deadlines for each step of your plan. Identify the resources you need to overcome the obstacle.

Seek Support: Share your challenges with a trusted friend, family member, or mentor. Connect with others who are facing similar challenges. If needed, consult with a therapist or counselor for guidance.

Stay Positive: Focus on the positive aspects of your life. Replace negative thoughts with positive affirmations. Imagine yourself overcoming the obstacle and achieving your goals.

Learn from Mistakes: Understand the reasons behind your setbacks. Use your mistakes as opportunities to learn and grow. Focus on the lessons you can learn from your mistakes.

Adapt and Adjust: Be willing to adjust your plans as needed. If one approach doesn't work, try another. By following these strategies, you can overcome obstacles and achieve your goals. Staying persistent, resilient, and focused on your ultimate objective is essential.

The Importance of Resilience and Perseverance

Resilience and perseverance are essential qualities for overcoming challenges and achieving Success. Resilience is the ability to bounce back from setbacks and adversity, while perseverance is the determination to continue progressing despite obstacles. These qualities are crucial for navigating the ups and downs of life and achieving your goals. Resilient individuals can cope with stress, maintain a positive outlook, and learn from mistakes. They view challenges as opportunities for growth and development rather than as insurmountable obstacles.

By developing resilience and perseverance, you can overcome any challenge that comes your way. Remember, Success often requires overcoming setbacks and persevering through difficulties. These qualities are essential for achieving your dreams and living a fulfilling life.

Chapter 2

Goal Setting and Achievement

2.1 Setting SMART Goals

SMART goals are a powerful tool for setting and achieving objectives. The acronym SMART stands for:

Specific: Your goal should be clear and well-defined. Avoid vague or general statements.

Measurable: You should be able to quantify your goal. This helps you track progress and stay motivated.
Achievable: Your goal should be realistic and attainable. Set goals that challenge you but are not overwhelming.
Time-bound: Set a deadline for your goal. This creates a sense of urgency and helps you stay focused.

Examples of SMART Goals

Here are some examples of SMART goals for different areas of life:

Career Goals: I will increase my salary by 15% within the next 12 months. I will obtain a PMP certification by the end of the year. I will network with at least 5 industry professionals in my field this quarter. My goal aligns with my career aspirations of becoming a project manager.

Health Goals: I will lose 10 pounds by my next doctor's appointment. I will exercise for at least 30 minutes, 5 times a week. My goal is realistic based on my current fitness level and lifestyle. My goal aligns with my desire to improve my overall health and well-being. I will reach my weight loss goal by the end of the year.

Personal Goals: I will read 12 books this year. I will practice yoga for 30 minutes 3 times a week. My goal is realistic based on my current schedule and interests. My goal aligns with my desire to improve my mental and emotional health. I will complete my reading goal by the end of the year.

Benefits of Setting SMART Goals

Setting SMART goals offers numerous advantages to help you achieve your desired outcomes. SMART goals provide a clear direction and purpose, boosting motivation and driving you towards your objectives. SMART goals help you stay accountable and track your progress, making it easier to stay on track. Achieving SMART goals can lead to a sense of accomplishment and satisfaction, boosting your self-esteem and confidence. SMART goals can help you make better decisions by aligning your actions with your priorities. You can improve your time management skills by setting deadlines and breaking down goals into smaller steps.

> *SMART goals can help you develop resilience by providing a framework for overcoming challenges and setbacks. When you have clear goals, it's easier to communicate your expectations to others, such as*

colleagues, team members, or loved ones. Setting SMART goals is a powerful tool that can help you achieve your desired outcomes and live a more fulfilling life.

2.2 Creating a Roadmap

Breaking down goals into smaller, achievable steps is essential for making them seem less daunting and increasing your chances of Success. Smaller steps can make your goals feel more manageable and less overwhelming, boosting your motivation. Breaking down your goals allows you to track your progress more quickly and celebrate small victories. When you break down your goals, you can anticipate potential challenges and develop strategies to overcome them. A well-defined plan helps you stay focused on your objectives and avoid distractions.

Techniques for creating a step-by-step plan

Mind mapping: Visualize your goals and the steps involved using a mind map.

Timeline: Create a timeline to set deadlines for each plan step.

Backward chaining: Start by imagining the final outcome and work backward to determine the steps needed to achieve it.

SMART goal breakdown: Break down your larger goal into smaller SMART goals.

Prioritization: Determine the most critical steps and prioritize them accordingly. Creating a clear and actionable plan can increase your chances of achieving your goals and staying on track.

Emphasizing Flexibility and Adaptability in Goal Planning

While a well-structured plan is essential for achieving your goals, it's equally important to be flexible and adaptable. Life can be unpredictable, and unexpected circumstances may arise that require you to adjust your plans. Recognize that things may not always go according to plan. Be open to making adjustments as needed. Consider potential obstacles and develop contingency plans. View setbacks as learning opportunities rather than failures. Periodically review your goals and make necessary adjustments. If your original plan doesn't work out, be willing to pivot and try a different approach.

By being flexible and adaptable, you can increase your chances of Success and overcome challenges that may arise along the way. Remember, the journey to achieving your goals is often filled with twists and turns, so it's essential to be prepared to adjust your course as needed.

2.3 Staying Focused and Motivated

Staying focused and motivated can be challenging, especially when faced with setbacks or distraction. Visualize your goals and visually represent your desired future. This can be a powerful motivator and help you focus on your objectives. Share your goals with friends, family, or colleagues who can provide support and encouragement. Someone holding you accountable can help you stay motivated and on track. Celebrate your achievements and reward yourself for reaching milestones. This can help you stay motivated and excited about your goals. Replace negative thoughts with positive affirmations. Remind yourself of your capabilities and the reasons why you're pursuing your goals. Create a conducive environment for productivity and minimize distractions that can hinder your progress.

Positive reinforcement

Positive reinforcement is a powerful technique for staying motivated. It involves rewarding yourself for positive behaviors or achievements. This can help you create a positive feedback loop and increase your motivation to continue working towards your goals. By incorporating these strategies into your routine, you can stay focused, motivated, and on track toward achieving your goals.

Overcoming Setbacks and Maintaining Motivation

Setbacks are a natural part of the journey to achieving your goals. Preparing to face challenges and develop strategies to maintain motivation is essential. Understand that setbacks are inevitable. Don't let them derail your progress. View setbacks as opportunities for growth and learning. Analyze what went wrong and make adjustments to your plan. Focus on the positive aspects of your situation and avoid dwelling on negativity. Be kind to yourself and avoid self-criticism. Talk to friends, family, or a mentor for support and encouragement. If a setback is significant, reassess your goals and make necessary adjustments.

By developing resilience and perseverance, you can overcome setbacks and maintain motivation to achieve your goals. Remember, setbacks are temporary; with the right mindset and strategies, you can overcome them and continue moving forward.

2.4 Celebrating Success

Celebrating your achievements is essential for maintaining motivation and staying on track towards your goals. Recognizing and rewarding your progress creates a positive feedback loop that can fuel your enthusiasm and drive. Celebrating your accomplishments can increase your motivation and keep you going. Recognizing your achievements can boost your self-confidence and self-esteem. Celebrating your progress makes you more likely to persevere through challenges. Recognizing and celebrating your achievements can create a positive and motivating environment to help you stay on track and achieve your goals.

The Benefits of Positive Reinforcement

Positive reinforcement is a powerful tool for motivating and encouraging desired behaviors. It involves rewarding positive actions or achievements to increase the likelihood that they will be repeated in the future. Positive reinforcement can significantly boost motivation and drive towards achieving goals. When people feel rewarded for their efforts, they are likelier to persist and continue working hard. Recognizing and rewarding positive behaviors can boost self-esteem and confidence. This can lead to a more positive outlook and greater self-worth. Positive reinforcement can strengthen relationships by fostering a positive and supportive environment. When people feel appreciated and valued, they are more likely to develop strong bonds with others. Positive reinforcement can help reduce stress and anxiety by creating a more positive and enjoyable experience. Positive reinforcement is a valuable tool for creating a positive and motivating environment.

Ideas for Celebrating Successes

Celebrating your achievements, both big and small, is essential for maintaining motivation and staying on track towards your goals. Here are some ideas for celebrating your successes:

Small Victories: Enjoy a small treat like a favorite snack, a ourelaxing bath, or a favorite activity. Share achievement with loved ones and enjoy a simple celebration. Reflect on your accomplishment and express your gratitude. Set up a reward system for yourself, such as earning points for each goal you achieve.

Significant Achievements: Take a trip, go out to dinner, or attend a concert. Treat yourself to a special gift or purchase. Celebrate your achievement with friends and family. Give back to others as a way to celebrate your Success. Create a physical reminder of your accomplishments, such as a framed certificate or a photo.

The most important thing is to find a way to celebrate that works for you and makes you feel good. The goal is to reinforce positive behaviors and create a positive and motivating environment.

Chapter 3

Building a Support System

3.1 The Importance of Relationships

Strong relationships are essential for our overall well-being. Friends, family, and mentors can provide invaluable support, encouragement, and guidance throughout our lives. They can offer a listening ear, a shoulder to cry on, and a source of motivation. Friends provide companionship, laughter, and a sense of belonging. They can offer advice, support, and encouragement during both good and bad times. Family members are often our closest confidants and supporters. They can provide unconditional love, guidance, and a sense of belonging. Mentors can offer valuable advice, guidance, and support based on their own experiences. They can help you navigate challenges, develop new skills, and achieve your goals.

Benefits of a Strong Support System

Strong relationships can help reduce stress and anxiety by providing a sense of belonging and support. Positive relationships can boost your mood and improve your overall quality of life. A robust support system can help you cope with challenges and setbacks more effectively. Strong relationships can reduce feelings of loneliness and isolation, which can positively impact your mental health. By nurturing solid relationships with friends, family, and mentors, you can create a supportive network to help you navigate life's challenges and achieve your goals.

The Importance of Building Healthy Relationships

Building healthy relationships is essential for our overall well-being. Both parties treat each other with respect and dignity. There is open and honest communication between the parties. The parties trust and rely on each other. The parties provide support and encouragement for each other. Both parties are willing to compromise and find common ground.

By building healthy relationships with friends, family, and mentors, you can create a supportive network to help you navigate life's challenges and achieve your goals. Remember, healthy relationships are based on mutual respect, open communication, trust, support, and compromise.

3.2 Finding Your Tribe

Finding your "tribe" – a community of like-minded people and professionally grow. When you surround yourself with people who share your interests and values, you create a supportive network that can offer encouragement, guidance, and opportunities.

Benefits of joining communities or groups

Being part of a community can provide a sense of belonging and support. You'll have people who understand your challenges and can offer encouragement and advice. Communities and groups can be great places to network and meet new people. This can lead to professional opportunities and friendships. Sharing experiences with others who understand your challenges can be comforting and validating.

Tips for finding like-minded people

Identify your interests: What are you passionate about? What are your hobbies or interests?

Join clubs or organizations: Look for clubs or organizations related to your interests.

Attend events: Attend events or meetups related to your interests.

Use social media: Join online communities or groups related to your interests.

Attend workshops or classes: Taking classes or seminars related to your interests can help you meet like-minded people. By actively seeking out communities and groups that align with your interests, you can create a supportive network that can enrich your life and help you achieve your goals.

Exploring Online Communities and Social Media Platforms

In today's digital age, online communities and social media platforms have become essential tools for connecting with people from all walks of life. These platforms offer many opportunities to find like-minded individuals, join groups, and participate in discussions on various topics. From Facebook and Reddit to LinkedIn and Twitter, countless options exist. By using online communities and social media, you can expand your network, connect with people who share your interests, and discover new opportunities for personal and professional growth.

It's essential to use these platforms responsibly and mindfully. Be respectful of others, protect your personal information, and engage in meaningful discussions. By doing so, you can create a positive and enriching online experience

3.3 Seeking Help

If you're struggling with overwhelming feelings, self-harm, substance abuse, relationship difficulties, or challenges, it's essential to seek professional Help. A therapist or counselor can provide you with the support and guidance you need to overcome these issues. When seeking professional help, it's important to find a therapist with whom you feel comfortable and qualified to address your specific needs. Seeking Help is a sign of strength, not weakness. You can improve your mental health and well-being by reaching out for support.

Types of Therapy and Counseling

There are many different types of therapy and counseling available. Some common types include:

Individual therapy: One-on-one sessions with a therapist to address personal issues.

Group therapy: Sessions with a group of people who are experiencing similar challenges.

Family therapy involves family members to address issues within the family unit.

Couples therapy: Therapy for couples to address relationship issues.

Cognitive-behavioral therapy (CBT): A type of therapy that focuses on changing negative thought patterns and behaviors. **Psychotherapy**: A broad term that encompasses many
different types of therapy. When seeking professional Help, you must find a therapist you feel comfortable with and who is qualified to address your specific needs.

The Importance of Self-Care and Seeking Help

Self-care is essential for maintaining our overall well-being. It involves taking care of our physical, mental, and emotional health. When we neglect our self-care, we are more likely to experience stress, anxiety, and burnout. Seeking Help when needed is a sign of strength, not weakness. It shows that we are taking responsibility for our mental health and well-being.

Taking care of yourself is not selfish. It's essential for your overall well-being and happiness. If you're struggling with mental health issues, don't hesitate to seek professional Help. There are many resources available to support you.

3.4 The Power of Giving Back

Volunteering and helping others benefits those in need and has significant positive impacts on the volunteers themselves.

Benefits of volunteering

Helping others can boost your mood and improve your overall quality of life. Volunteering can increase your sense of self-worth and accomplishment. Volunteering can help you build stronger relationships with others. Volunteering can help you develop new skills and enhance existing ones. By volunteering, you can make a positive difference in your community.

Volunteer opportunities

Countless volunteer opportunities are available, ranging from local charities to international organizations. Here are a few examples:

Animal shelters: Volunteer to care for animals, walk dogs, or help with other tasks.

Hospitals or nursing homes: Volunteer to visit with patients or assist with daily tasks.

Environmental organizations: Participate in conservation efforts or environmental cleanup projects.

Community centers: Volunteer to help with various programs and activities.

Tutoring programs: Tutor children or adults in need of assistance. By volunteering, you can positively impact the world and enrich your own life. It's rewarding to give back to your community and make a difference.

The Importance of Giving Back to Your Community

Giving back to your community is a powerful way to impact and enrich your life positively. Volunteering your time and resources can help address critical social and environmental issues and create a more vibrant and equitable community. Helping others can give you a sense of purpose and meaning in your life. Volunteering can help you build stronger relationships with your community members. Giving back can help you develop new skills and learn valuable lessons.

Volunteering can help address critical social and environmental issues and positively impact your community.

Giving back to your community can create a more compassionate and caring world. It's a rewarding way to make a difference and enrich your own life.

Chapter 4

Self-Care and Well-being

4.1 Taking Care of Yourself

Our overall well-being is a delicate balance of physical, mental, and emotional health. Neglecting any one of these aspects can have a significant impact on our quality of life. Taking care of our bodies is essential for our overall well-being. Regular exercise, a healthy diet, and adequate sleep are crucial for maintaining good physical health. Our mental health plays a vital role in our thinking, feeling, and behavior. It's essential to pay attention to our mental health and seek help when needed. Our emotional health involves managing our emotions and coping with life's challenges. It's essential to develop healthy coping mechanisms and seek support when needed.

Benefits of Self-Care

Self-care can help manage stress and anxiety levels. Engaging in self-care activities can boost your mood and improve your overall well-being. Taking care of your physical and mental health can increase your energy levels. You're more likely to be productive when you're well-rested and taking care of yourself. Self-care can help you build and maintain healthy relationships.

Tips for Incorporating Self-Care into Your Daily Routine

- Prioritize sleep
- Eat a healthy diet Exercise regularly Manage stress Spend time in nature Limit screen time spend time with loved ones Pursue hobbies and interests:

By prioritizing self-care, you can improve your overall well-being and live a more fulfilling life.

4.2 Stress Management Techniques

Young adults often face a variety of stressors, such as balancing schoolwork, exams, and extracurricular activities. Job hunting, career changes, and work-related stress. Challenges in personal or romantic relationships. Managing debt, tuition costs, and living expenses. They are feeling pressure to fit in or meet societal expectations.

Relaxation Techniques

Focus on the present moment without judgment. Pay attention to your thoughts, feelings, and sensations. Practice deep breathing and focus on a mantra or visualization. Inhale deeply through your nose, hold for a few seconds, and exhale slowly through your mouth. Tense and relax different muscle groups to reduce tension. Combine physical postures, breathing exercises, and meditation.

Time Management Strategies

Prioritize tasks: Identify the most important tasks and focus on completing them first. Use a planner or calendar to schedule your time effectively. Set achievable goals to avoid feeling overwhelmed. Focus on one task at a time to improve productivity. Short breaks can help you stay focused and avoid burnout. Incorporating these stress management techniques into your daily routine can effectively manage stress and improve your overall well-being.

4.3 Healthy Habits

A healthy lifestyle is essential for both physical and mental well-being. It involves maintaining a balanced diet, getting enough sleep, and engaging in regular physical activity. Nutrition is crucial in providing our bodies with the necessary nutrients to function optimally. A balanced diet includes a variety of foods from all food groups, such as fruits, vegetables, grains, protein sources, and dairy. Sleep is equally important for overall health and well-being. Exercise is another crucial component of a healthy lifestyle. Exercise can help you feel more energized and alert. Regular exercise can reduce your risk of heart disease and stroke. You can improve your overall health and well-being by prioritizing nutrition, sleep, and exercise.

Tips for Eating a Healthy Diet

Consume various foods from all food groups, including fruits, vegetables, grains, protein sources, and dairy. Be mindful of portion sizes to avoid overeating. Reduce your intake of processed foods, which are often high in unhealthy fats, sugars, and sodium. Drink plenty of water throughout the day. Pay attention to the nutritional information on food labels. Pay attention to your body's hunger and fullness cues.

Tips for Getting Enough Sleep

Ensure your bedroom is dark, quiet, and calm. Go to bed and wake up at the same time each day. Avoid caffeine and alcohol close to bedtime. The blue light emitted by electronic devices can interfere with sleep. Engage in calming activities before bed, such as reading or taking a warm bath. If you're struggling with sleep, consult a healthcare professional.

Encouraging Regular Physical Activity

Choose activities that you find fun. Start with achievable goals and gradually increase the intensity and duration of your workouts. Incorporate physical activity into your daily routine. Exercising with a friend can make it more enjoyable and motivating. Try different types of exercise to prevent boredom and target various muscle groups.

4.4 Finding Balance

Achieving a healthy work-life balance is essential for overall well-being and Success. It involves effectively managing your time and prioritizing your commitments to ensure that you have enough time for work, school, and personal life.

Tips for Time Management and Prioritizing Tasks Use a

planner or calendar to schedule your time effectively. Break down large tasks into smaller, more manageable steps. Identify the most important tasks and focus on completing them first. Allocate specific time blocks for different activities. If possible, delegate tasks to others to reduce your workload. Focus on one task at a time to improve productivity.

Work-Life Balance

Work-life balance is about finding a healthy equilibrium between your professional and personal life. It means not sacrificing your personal well-being for the sake of your career or studies. Establish clear boundaries between work and personal time. Make time for activities that you enjoy and that help you relax. Avoid working excessive hours and take time off when needed. Don't be afraid to say no to additional commitments if you're already overwhelmed.

You can reduce stress, improve your overall well-being, and achieve your goals by effectively managing your time, prioritizing your tasks, and finding a healthy balance between work, school, and personal life.

Chapter 5

Inspiring Stories and Role Models

5.1 The Power of Inspiration

Inspiring stories have the power to motivate, encourage, and uplift us. They can ignite our passions, spark our creativity, and encourage us to pursue our dreams. By sharing the experiences of others who have overcome challenges and achieved Success, we can learn valuable lessons and gain the motivation to persevere.

The Psychology of Inspiration

Inspiration is a complex psychological phenomenon that involves a combination of factors. We are more likely to be inspired by people who we can relate to or identify with. Inspiring stories can give us hope and belief in our own potential. Inspiration can ignite our motivation and drive us to achieve our goals.

The Influence of Role Models

Role models are individuals who inspire us and serve as positive examples. They can influence our behavior, beliefs, and values in significant ways. By observing and learning from role models, we can develop our own skills, qualities, and aspirations. Role models can provide us with many things. They can offer advice, support, and mentorship. They can inspire us to achieve our goals and overcome challenges. They can motivate us to strive for excellence

5.2 Famous Role Models

Throughout history, countless individuals have faced adversity and overcome tremendous challenges to achieve extraordinary Success. These individuals serve as powerful role models, inspiring us to persevere and reach our own goals.

Examples of famous individuals who overcame challenges and achieved Success

Nelson Mandela: Imprisoned for 27 years for his opposition to apartheid, Mandela emerged from prison to become the first democratically elected president of South Africa.

Oprah Winfrey: Overcoming poverty, abuse, and discrimination, Oprah Winfrey became one of the most influential women in the world.

J.K. Rowling: Rejected by countless publishers, J.K. Rowling persevered to become the author of the bestselling Harry Potter series.

Stephen Hawking: Despite being diagnosed with ALS at a young age, Stephen Hawking became a renowned physicist and author.

Grit and Resilience: The Keys to Success

Grit and resilience are two essential qualities that can help us overcome challenges and achieve our goals. Grit is the passion and perseverance for long-term goals. It's the ability to stick with something even when it's challenging. Resilience is the ability to bounce back from adversity and continue moving forward. Both grit and resilience are essential for achieving Success. By cultivating these qualities, we can overcome challenges, persevere through setbacks, and ultimately achieve our goals.

5.3 Everyday Heroes

While famous individuals often capture our attention, it's essential to recognize the extraordinary contributions of everyday heroes in our communities. These unsung heroes are positively impacting the world around us, often without seeking recognition.

Examples of Everyday Heroes

Educators who inspire their students and shape their lives. Nurses, doctors, and other healthcare professionals who dedicate their lives to caring for others. Firefighters, police officers, and paramedics who risk their lives to protect our communities. Individuals who dedicate their time and energy to helping others. People who are actively involved in their communities and making a positive impact.

Recognizing and Celebrating Everyday Heroes

Everyday heroes are the unsung individuals who positively impact our communities, often without seeking recognition. They are the teachers who inspire their students, the healthcare workers who dedicate their lives to caring for others, the volunteers who give their time to help those in need and the community leaders who work tirelessly to improve their neighborhoods. By recognizing and celebrating everyday heroes, we can inspire others to make a difference, show our appreciation for their contributions, encourage them to continue their work, and foster a sense of unity and belonging in our communities.

Finding Inspiration in Your Own Community

Our communities are filled with inspiring individuals making a positive difference daily. Looking around us, we can find countless examples of everyday heroes dedicated to helping others, improving their communities, and making the world a better place. By seeking inspiration in your community, you can discover countless examples of individuals who are making a difference and find motivation to make a positive impact yourself. Let's inspire each other to create a better world.

5.4 Becoming Your Own Hero

One of the most powerful forces within us is our own belief in ourselves and our potential. We are more likely to overcome challenges, persevere through setbacks, and achieve our goals when we believe in ourselves.

The Importance of Self-Belief and Self-Confidence

Self-belief and self-confidence are essential for Success. They provide us with the motivation, determination, and resilience to overcome obstacles and achieve our dreams. We are more willing to step outside our comfort zone and try new things. We are more likely to persist through challenges and setbacks. We are more likely to achieve our goals when we believe in our ability.

How to Develop Self-Belief and Self-Confidence

Replace negative thoughts with positive affirmations. Recognize and celebrate your successes, no matter how small. Set goals that are challenging but attainable. Spend time with people who support and encourage you. If you're struggling with self-esteem or self-confidence, consider seeking professional Help.

Tips for Developing a Positive Self-Image

A positive self-image is essential for overall well-being and Success. Here are some tips for developing a positive self-image:

Challenge negative thoughts: Identify and challenge negative thoughts about yourself. Replace them with positive affirmations.

Focus on your strengths: Acknowledge and celebrate your strengths and accomplishments.

Practice self-compassion: Be kind to yourself and avoid self-criticism.

Practice self-care: Take care of your physical, mental, and emotional health. By incorporating these tips into your daily life, you can develop a positive self-image and boost your confidence and self-belief.

Conclusion

Throughout this book, we have explored various aspects of motivation, goal setting, self-care, and personal growth. We have discussed the importance of understanding your motivations, setting SMART goals, building a solid support system, practicing self-care, and finding inspiration in others. Your journey to self-discovery and fulfilment is unique, and there is no one-size-fits-all approach. The key is to see what works best for you and to stay committed to your goals. By incorporating the strategies and techniques outlined in this book, you can ignite your inner fire and achieve your dreams. Remember, every journey starts with a single step. Take that step today and watch your life transform. Understand your motivations and find ways to stay motivated. Create clear, achievable goals to guide your progress. Surround yourself with positive and supportive people. Take care of your physical, mental, and emotional health. Seek inspiration from others and believe in yourself. Believe in yourself, stay motivated, and never abandon your dreams. You can achieve anything you want with dedication, perseverance, and a positive mindset.

M.J.Moon author central links-
https://www.amazon.com/author/moonbook99

www.ingramcontent.com/pod-product-compliance
Lightning Source LLC
Chambersburg PA
CBHW061345040426
42444CB00011B/3095